Saying Hello...

to Life

By Sherri Heath

Chapters

DEDICATION

Dedicated to those who take the second chance at life, and find it.

Introduction

Living our lives day after day, routines and schedules are made. Lifelong plans are carefully thought out and we have in our minds how we think our life will be and envision how it will go as we journey through it. Occasionally, we hit a bump or two, and think it's just temporary and life will get back on track again as we planned. My 'bump' in the road completely put me on a new journey in my life. I had to decide to move forward, or try to get back on the track that didn't even exist anymore. I chose to move forward. There really wasn't even an option….

My husband of 34 years died from cancer after a year and a half battle. I became a widow at the age of 53. My life stopped evolving with joy, peace, laughter, hope and happiness. My journey of grief healing can be found in my first book, 'Saying Goodbye from Death to Life'.

We can find joy in living again after life changes our direction of what we thought was the perfect life. The bumps that create havoc and hardships can be smoothed out and a new path created. Just listen to the voice of the Creator and all that is good in this life. Leave the battles of the past, in the past. Close the door, lock it and never return. Maybe the first time around with life all the planned out ideas and hopes just fell from under you and the path now is unclear. Well, I can tell you, sometimes you have to make a new path and grab hold of all you have left of your hope and joy and press forward!

This little book tells stories of discovering a 'second chance' to experience joy, peace, laughter, hope and happiness again. Enjoy, and smile as you hear me 'Saying Hello to… Life.'

Chapter one

PEACE

~Freedom from disturbances; quiet and tranquility~

35th Wedding Anniversary

"To give light to those who sit in darkness and the shadow of death, to guide our feet into the way of peace."
Luke 1:79

Who has been married at least 35 years? Well, I barely missed it. I was married 34 years, 7 months and 14 days to my high school sweetheart. On January 16, 2014, I became a widow. LIFE stopped, or so I thought.

So here's my anniversary date on June 2nd and I no longer had my husband. What does a widow at the age of 53 do? I certainly didn't want to be around people. I needed to sort this out. I had already said my goodbyes to my husband to a degree that I was starting to heal from my grief and loss. God had come to me and comforted me and I had accepted His peace and hope for my future. But then there's this 35th anniversary thing…the date was getting closer and I was starting to feel some anxiety about it. I've never NOT celebrated our wedding day. What to do, what to do….the lost feeling started creeping back into my being.

I decided to plan a weekend getaway. My sister-in-law's city was holding a music festival, so I decided to drive there on a Friday evening and enjoy the festivities Friday night and Saturday. I booked a hotel in Tulsa for Saturday night and scheduled a few hours at a spa for Sunday. I was nervous about doing all this, especially because my mind and heart were battling with the absence of my husband for this trip.

I gathered my items for a two night stay. Then I thought I might pack some birthday and anniversary cards that my husband had given me. Who does this? I think many women are sentimental enough to hang on to keepsake cards and notes. Then I discovered letters from my husband that I kept while he was in Navy boot camp. Goodness, they were close to 30 years old. I didn't even open them; I just shoved them in a big envelope along with some of the cards. I tossed my bag in the car and headed north toward Tulsa.

I wasn't sure what awaited me, but my sister-in-law and her husband welcomed me with excitement and hugs. I had drawn very close to her during my husband's illness. My husband's older sister, she helped a great deal with his care.

She and I walked to the festival that evening, ate at the food booths and sat in the twilight listening to several different bands. It was a very relaxed evening with a person who shared the same great loss.

The next morning, we headed back out and walked the festival grounds, shopped at craft booths, talked and laughed and truly enjoyed our time together under different circumstances. That afternoon, I said my goodbyes and left for Tulsa.

I arrived too early to check in, so I drove to the mall. I remembered walking in this same mall with my husband years before on an anniversary weekend. We bought a pasta machine together as our gift. I shopped a little, but didn't buy anything except a bottle of champagne.

I really like champagne and after all, it was my anniversary!

I headed back to my hotel. Located on the 10th floor, I opened the shades and saw a nice view of the city. I wasn't sure what to do next. I turned on the TV, unpacked my bag and hung up my clothes. I even put my undies in the dresser drawer, like I was planning to stay for a week.

I called a pizza place for delivery of a large veggie pizza, with no green bell peppers. I wandered down the hall with my ice bucket and put my champagne on ice. Then I waited. Waited for the pizza delivery. Waited to face my 35th wedding anniversary…alone.

The knock at the door startled me. I peeked out to see if it was the pizza delivery and of course it was. I still felt nervous about spending the night in a big hotel in the city all alone. The loneliness tried to seep back into my thoughts….

I popped the cork on my champagne, opened the pizza and lay across the bed with the big envelope of letters and cards next to me. I ate a piece of pizza, sipped champagne, then ate another piece…sipped more champagne. I was fighting with opening the envelope.

I sat my glass of champagne down, turned some music on, slowly opened the envelope and spilled all the contents out on the bed. I was anxious to read the letters first. I organized them by date and read the oldest one first, tears already starting to run down my face. I knew this would be hard, but I felt like I needed to do this. I started reading, out loud, sipped champagne and read the second one out loud. Seeing his handwriting comforted me, as if he was somehow there with me in the room. It had been awhile since I had seen his writing. The letters were just about what he was doing, how he missed us all and wanted me to send pictures of me and our little daughter. He encouraged me that the weeks would soon pass and we would start our new life with his Navy career. "We can do this; it's only a temporary separation." I continued to read, but not out loud anymore. Tears were streaming down my cheeks now, and I could not speak them out loud. I read each letter, and then gently returned them to the big envelope. I just sat there, crying uncontrollably. Sadness swept over me like a waterfall…covering me to the point I could hardly breathe.

After a bit, I got up, washed my face, poured a fresh glass of sweet champagne and sat down next to the cards. Did I want to continue? Yes, I must. Why had I kept these cards? Was it for this purpose? To read the words of how he felt about me on birthdays, anniversaries and sweet little cards of 'just because'? My mind began to spin in circles. I said out loud, "You're not here. You're not here anymore. I won't ever get cards like this again from you! I will never see or hear how you feel about me, us. I'm alone. You left me! You are gone! You left me! Why did you go?" I felt so angry and upset that this terrible thing had happened to me. I cried and yelled, threw the pillows off the bed and then ripped the blankets off, hurling them to the floor. Everything inside me hurt. The pain of being alone and lost was so intense that I fell across the bed and sobbed again.

After a while, I started reading the rest of the cards. Some were funny, some serious. A smile came to my face as I finished reading the last birthday card and put it away in the big envelope. I knew how he had felt about me. I knew he had loved me. I knew he didn't want to leave me all alone. I pushed the pizza box and the big envelope to the other side of the bed and curled up under the covers. All was quiet. All was well with my soul. Peace came and I fell asleep.

"I will both lie down in peace, and sleep; for you alone, O Lord, make me dwell in safety."
– Psalm 4:8

"Peace I leave with you, my peace I give to you; not as the world gives do I give to you. Let not your heart be troubled, neither let it be afraid." - John 14:27

I woke the next morning, peaceful. I started packing up all my things and cleaning up the room since I had flung things around the night before. I laughed to myself thinking the maids will wonder what kind of party the occupant of this room had. I checked out and headed to my spa appointment.

If you haven't ever been to a spa, you need to go. What a treat to be pampered into total relaxation. First I had a full body massage. The room was dimly lit and tranquil, soothing music played. I closed my eyes as the masseuse kneaded the tight muscles in my back. I totally relaxed. It felt like she was rubbing all the emotions from the night before out of me. It was such a release that my eyes became teary. After the massage, I had a body wrap treatment. My face, hands and feet were covered with warm towels as I lay very still wrapped in herbs. I literally felt like I was floating! What a wonderful, relaxing few hours. I was renewed!

I left Tulsa and headed back home. I felt extremely proud of myself for surviving the weekend and had the most peaceful spirit inside me. God's Grace and peace had touched me and pushed out the fear, loneliness and sadness. He allowed me to work through it, and I know He was with me in that hotel room. I'm pretty sure I fell asleep with His arms wrapped around me. I had hope for the days ahead because I had happiness and peace in my heart.

"For you shall go out with joy, and be led out with peace; the mountains and hills shall break forth into singing before you, and all the trees of the field shall clap their hands.-Isaiah 55:12

Chapter Two

JOY

~A feeling of great pleasure and happiness- rejoice~

NEW GRANDAUGHTER

"And my soul shall be joyful in the Lord; it shall rejoice in His salvation." – Psalm 35:9

What an honor to become a grandma, to have grandkids to spoil! My daughter became pregnant and told my husband and I in October with a little gift bag holding a cute onesie with a pumpkin on it. What a surprise! They had been married for about two years and were so excited and full of joy. I lost my husband to cancer just three months after she announced her pregnancy. That was very hard for her, but she knew the blessing she carried and they were anxious to become a family.

We held the baby reveal party with the blue and pink cake and all the cute baby decorations. It was exciting to see them cut the cake and find out if they were having a girl or boy. It revealed pink! Oh, the excitement! I was going to have a granddaughter! I had three handsome grandsons already, so it was time to add a girl to the mix! We shared happy tears and heartfelt hugs.

Then came the baby showers. Oh my, did they get showered! Between church, family and friends, they received everything they needed to start life with their little girl. The fun part was playing the games…one in particular was to diaper a baby doll blind folded. Everyone laughed when both grandmas competed against each other! We all had such a good time. The gifts they received were placed in the baby nursery that she had carefully decorated and detailed. She was ready to hold this baby in her arms.

All the while I was anticipating the arrival, sorrow still lingered in my heart that my husband was not able to share this incredible event. This baby would never know her grandpa. This is the little girl that was supposed to wrap him around her little finger and be spoiled rotten by him. She would miss out on all that…It's funny how our minds tend to create situations that will never happen.

All I know is that I AM here; I'm the grandma that can spoil her. I'm the grandma that can laugh with her and build memories with. I would be that grandma! Did I still feel alone? Yes. But I knew this little girl was precious and needed to know the joy that a Grandparent can give!

I received the call on an early Sunday morning; they were on their way to the hospital. It was time! The hospital is about one and a half hours from my house. So by the time I arrived, she was already in her room all wired up. Her labor pains were still mild. She walked up and down the halls, sat on the big yoga ball and did everything right to get her labor moving. Every time she did the right things, the baby's heart would slow way down. The nurses told her to just stay in bed and let the labor take its course that way. That concerned me, but the nurses assured it wasn't unusual.

A little later, the machines she was wired up to started beeping loudly and the nurse ran in to check. The baby's heart rate dropped drastically! They repositioned my daughter on the bed and the baby's heart rate improved. When the nurse left, the beeping alarms sounded off again.

This scenario went on for a while. The doctor soon arrived and examined her. He announced that they needed to do an emergency cesarean because the baby's heart rate was not staying steady. He wasn't willing to take the risk of anything going wrong.

Oh my! Well, that suddenly changed everything! The joyful anticipation for the birth of this baby suddenly became a scary concern! My daughter started crying and shaking. She was so scared and shocked that her birth experience was changing into something she wasn't prepared for. Her husband started putting on the hospital 'garb' to accompany her during the surgery. The nurses saw him and told him he could not go. They had to put her completely under anesthesia for the procedure. She was already scared of needles, and never had anesthesia before.

We all said our goodbyes to her as they quickly wheeled her out of the room toward the double doors at the end of the long hallway. Her sweet husband held her hand all the way to the doors. Then he stood there peeking between the cracks of the doors trying to see her. My heart just sank for him. I put my arms around him and hugged tightly. We shed tears and prayed together. He refused to leave and stayed by the doors until he heard word from the nurses.

Not knowing is one of the hardest things to deal with. Conversations were quiet and calls were made to family and friends. Minutes turned to hours. Worry had set in. The 'what ifs' started to take over in our minds. Prayers started sounding like pleas. What was going on in there? Why hadn't we heard anything? Suddenly, a nurse opened the doors and asked her husband to get his scrubs back on and come in the room. We struggled as fast as we could to get them on him, and he quickly disappeared behind the doors.

We all went to the nursery viewing windows to see if we could see the new baby. She wasn't in there. We waited and waited. Concerns were building and no nurses were available to ask what was going on.

Finally, they brought my daughter to her room, groggy and sleepy. I was so thankful that she was okay. The nurse told us the baby had a few issues and was in observation. They told us we could see her in the nursery, but only through an area where they would lift the curtain. We all gathered around a little window in the back hallway of the nursery. There she was, a little baby girl with a full head of dark hair. She was wired up, had an IV and was lying under the warm lights of her tiny bed. What a beautiful child; what a beautiful blessing. What a release of worry.

My daughter was in her room crying. She hadn't seen or held her daughter yet. We saw the baby before she did! We talked to the head nurse and arranged for them to go into the nursery to see their new baby. It was the most precious moment to see as I viewed them from the porthole window. They hugged each other and touched their newborn infant carefully and gently as if she would break. They were still not allowed to hold her, but they spent time with her, talking softly and holding her teensy hand.

The doctor told my daughter and son-in-law that the baby was having trouble stabilizing blood sugar levels. They needed to keep her for a few days to get it leveled out. It was a deep sigh of relief.

The following afternoon, they brought my new little granddaughter to my daughter. She took her and held her close and cried. How hard it must have been to endure 24 hours before she could hold her new baby. We all cried. What joy it gave us to see this beautiful, new little girl snuggle in her momma's arms safe, warm and content. Then it was Grandma's turn! My heart leaped with joy as I held her and introduced myself as her grandma. So precious in His sight, so beautiful to hold and kiss. God's perfect timing for this birth; to bring joy to the family with new life when we had just lost life a few months before.

"for weeping may endure for a night, but joy
comes in the morning"
-Psalms 16:11

"Therefore you now have sorrow; but I will see you again
and your heart will rejoice, and your joy
no one will take from you."
-John 16:22

Chapter Three

HOPE

~A feeling of trust~

Pitter Patter Heart

"Return to the stronghold, you prisoners of hope. Even today I declare that I will restore double to you" – Zechariah 9:12

After my husband passed away, I was adjusting to working again and getting my financials in order. Life became busy enough to occupy most of my time. I had a new grandbaby to add to three grandsons and had a life long friend move in with me. She always said that we would end up living together in our old age. It's just sooner than expected! Life was plugging along at a pace I could handle. Experiencing the grief process is different for everyone, and I felt that God had touched me and I had accepted His peace in my loss. I was beginning to heal from my grief. It's a choice to move forward and find life, or stay stuck in grief to live in a very dark place with sorrow. I chose to move forward with the help of my heavenly Father.

Here I was, 53 years old and never been with any man other than my husband when I married at 18 years old. Dating wasn't even a notion. I knew I could be just fine and content with all my children, grandchildren, family and friends at this time in my life. I had a good marriage of nearly 35 years, and a wonderful family as the result.

Remember the Bible story of Naomi and Ruth? Both were widows and both were blessed and taken care of. I had read a book written from a widow about Naomi and Ruth. It was truly inspiring and brought hope that God can provide people in our lives that care for us.

I wasn't sure if I could continue the path I was on financially. My house payment was almost equal to the amount I brought home each month. My friend was very limited in helping me financially, but she loved to cook and she helped me in so many other ways. As I was trying to spreadsheet my bills and financial woes, I received a call from my aunt. She is a beautiful person with a talent for playing the fiddle. She played every Friday evening at a little country gathering of about 100 people. Different musicians played on stage with a variety of people coming up to sing. It's like 'live Karaoke.' The average age is probably around 70 years old. I occasionally attended because my parents, aunts and uncles all go and sing or play.

Well, her conversation on the phone surprised me. She told me she gave my number to a fella that came and played his guitar and sang some songs. She said he lost his wife and thought maybe we could get together and talk since we had widowhood in common. I chuckled and told her okay, I guess that would be alright. Thinking about the average age of this singing shindig, I didn't really see any harm in it.

Some time went by and then one Saturday mid-morning, I was getting dressed, ready to go to town for the day and the phone rang. I answered and in a deep, friendly voice with a southern drawl, he introduced himself. He told me my aunt gave him my phone number. I was in shock! I sat down slowly on my bed and tried to make sense of it all.

It had been over 35 years since I talked to another man about meeting up with him. Evidently, he was closer to my age than I thought!

He told me a funny story about my aunt. She had told him about me and said she would give him my number at intermission during the music shindig. She gave him a scrap of paper, which he shoved in his pocket. Later, after he was home, he pulled out the paper and it said; milk, bread, orange juice….It was her grocery list! He laughed and thought she must be a little 'off' or something. He didn't go back to the music event for several weeks, and when he did, she ran up to him and apologized for giving him her grocery list and this time gave him my number.

We decided to meet the following week at a family style restaurant after I got off work. I can't say how nervous I felt! I wasn't sure I really wanted to do this. A blind date basically set up by my aunt. So, I'm thinking my aunt was Naomi and I was playing the part of Ruth. Did I really want to meet someone new? I was doing fine, spending my days working and visiting grandkids on weekends. Just like Ruth, she was doing fine by going out, working in the fields and gathering food for her and Naomi. She obeyed Naomi and worked hard to make their life comfortable. Naomi knew the potential for a better life for Ruth, so she made sure Ruth was at the right place and the right time for Boaz to come by and take notice. Isn't God's timing wonderful? Sometimes when we least expect things, opportunities and situations are placed before us to experience. This first 'date' after 35 years was unexpected and a new experience!

Before I left work that day, I went to the ladies room and brushed my hair, dabbed my makeup a little and took several deep breaths. I was actually shaking! I drove to the restaurant and saw a man sitting on the bench out front. Oh boy, how do I do this!? I walked up to him; we introduced ourselves, went in and sat at a booth. The best way I can describe my first encounter with him was that I saw a tall, tan, very nice looking and very polite man. We sat across from each other. I felt so inadequate and a little shy. I thought his southern drawl was quite intriguing and enjoyed listening to him tell about who he was and what he did. We sat there and talked for about four hours, even after the restaurant closed and was being cleaned. We muddled through our dinner, told stories about our past and shared tears about our losses and laughter of our memories. We had a lot in common. He lost his wife two months prior to when I lost my husband. He had been married almost 38 years.

My heart went pitter patter when he smiled. Oh my! Was this my Boaz? Was this an unexpected meeting by mere coincidence? Or was this something that happened at the right time and at the right place in my life?

God allowed our paths to cross and we both knew this relationship was divine intervention. We shared common interests such as church, family, fishing and music. Neither of us liked being alone and neither of us were looking for a new relationship, but we ended up being together as we began to walk this new path that tragedy put us on. What a blessing to receive!

"Blessed is the man who trusts in the Lord, and whose hope is the Lord."
-Jeremiah 17:7

"Be of good courage, and He shall strengthen your heart,
all you who hope in the Lord"
-Psalm 31:24

Chapter 4

LAUGHTER

~A cause of merriment~

Gone Fishin'

"Blessed are you who weep now, for you shall laugh."- Luke 6:21

"He will yet fill your mouth with laughing, and your lips with rejoicing" – Job 8:21

I never thought I would find myself sitting in a Bass Boat in February (yes, there is fishing year around which I didn't have a clue about. I thought fishing was only for spring and summer!). I was bundled up in a down jacket, gloves, boots and my hood was tied so tight that I only had a peep-hole to see. It was the first fishing tournament with the Bass Masters of Chickasha in Oklahoma. We were a two-person team racing at top speed across the lake, before sunrise, in the dark, to 'the place,' the ultimate fishing spot. One of my gloves flew off as I tried to hold on to the handle in front of me. Cold water splashed and sprayed on me and all over the seats. The waves were at least two, four or maybe even 10 feet high! Well, it seemed to me like they were. It was thrilling, freezing and one of the best new experiences I've ever had. My team member was a gift from God. He had arranged our meeting and we both knew it was Divine intervention! Who would have thought?

He taught me how to prepare for the tournament by bringing in at least twenty fishing poles into the living room. We needed to replace the line, place bait (all artificial bait!) on them and make sure they were all in working order. I laughed to myself as we dragged all them into the house along with the containers of bait. I figured out pretty quick that this isn't fishing for just fun, but serious stuff! He was so patient with me showing me how to put new line on the reels and also about the different kinds of bait used for different kinds of conditions, such as water temperature, time of year, color of water and so on. I had no idea fishing was such a science!

So, here I was, sitting in a bass boat, fishing pole in hand with all the right bait rigged up. I sat on that little chair on the back and just chuckled thinking to myself, "What am I doing here?"

I just smiled and cast another cast as the cold rain drenches my clothes. We fished ALL day, eight hours and we didn't even catch one bass. Oh, but the thrill of it all. I was willing to step into a new adventure, not knowing what it takes to be in a competitive fishing tournament.

One time while fishing in a tournament it was stormy, with thunder and rain, but not close lightning, so we continued to fish. The temperature was warmer, early spring. I was wearing rain gear and the only thing that got too wet was my head. We were floating in a little cove near the end of the day and the rain had practically stopped. We just needed one more bass. We had four in the live well, but needed our quota of five. Suddenly, my fishing partner got a bite and was reeling. He hollered, "Fish! Fish!" I put down my rod, stumbled to get the net, leaned over and netted the big bass. We were so excited! It was our fifth fish and it was a good one. I turned around and low and behold, my brand new matching red rod and reel that I just bought at the big Bassmasters Pro Tournament Series in

Tulsa (like the Super bowl of fishing) just a few weeks before was GONE! Evidently I knocked it off the boat getting to the net. Oh! I was so disappointed and upset! Well, we had our five and basically, we were done, so I decided to go in after my rod and reel. The boat was sitting in about five feet of water, so I figured I could use the net and find it on the bottom. We took the boat to shore; I got out and stripped down to my undershirt and socks and slowly started to tiptoe into the lake. Brrrrr!! The water was NOT as warm as the air and in spring, it was still probably in the low 70's. There I was, up to my neck in lake water dragging the big net along the bottom. My partner laughed and I think he thought I was a bit crazy! I didn't care; I was determined to at least try and find my new rod. Needless to say, I didn't find it. My story is that a bigger bass got hold of my bait, pulled the rod off the boat and took off with it. I'm sticking with that story!

Watching the sun rise on the lake and seeing this man that God so graciously blessed me with, cast his fishing pole is all the winning I ever need. Live life fully.

He sends unexpected blessings as long as you are willing to look for and receive them. Laugh and roll with life!

"Then our mouth was filled with laughter, and our tongue with singing, then they said among the nations, "The Lord has done great things for them."

-Psalms 126:2

Chapter Five

HAPPINESS

~A feeling or pleasure and enjoyment because of your life~

Family Ties

"Happy is he who has the God of Jacob for his help, whose hope is in the Lord his God"
- Psalms 146:5

"Happy are the people who are in such a state: happy are the people whose God is the Lord!"
-Psalm 144:15

My husband passed away and went to heaven and left me at the age of 53 with three grown children, three beautiful grandsons and another grandchild on the way. Timing wasn't very good since we were finally empty nesters and looked forward to our 'golden years' together. But all that changed. We always cherished our family and children. That's one reason we decided to retire from Navy life and return back home where our parents and relatives lived.

Years before we retired, my husband's 16 year old nephew's Dad passed away suddenly and we decided to become his nephew's legal guardians. The boy's mother had died when he was nine months old, so we basically became his parents. He traveled with us to Sicily, Italy and lived with us as a part of our military family. What a privilege to have him with us! About a year older than my son, we suddenly had two teenage boys age 15 and 16, a 19 year old daughter and a 9 year old daughter all living in a three-bedroom military housing duplex. It was a challenge, but we made it work by converting the dining room into a bedroom for the youngest with a curtain across the doorway. The boys shared a room with bunkbeds and our older daughter had her own room. I always made it a point to eat dinner together at our crowded little table in the kitchen corner.

We moved back to Oklahoma and our nephew graduated high school and started college. We felt proud that we could help him start his life successfully as an adult by being a part of our family.

About three years before my husband passed away, my youngest daughter brought home her best friend from school. They had both just started their senior year of high school. They told me they needed to talk to me about something. I was busy in the kitchen and told them to go ahead. They asked me to come and sit down to talk. They were both teary eyed and my daughter told me that her friend's mother kicked her out of the house. She showed me bruises on her arm and the side of her face. I sat there in shock. Her friend had just turned 18 years old the month before, so she wasn't a minor anymore. I was thankful for that. Otherwise, I would have had to call the state agency. They asked if she could stay with us for a while. Of course she could stay with us!

I cleaned out our office, found a twin bed and fixed up the bookshelf for her clothes. My husband and I were thankful that we were able to help her and be there for her. Her mother ended up throwing all her clothes out on the front porch for her to pick up. She disowned her and hasn't contacted her since.

We sat down and talked with her letting her know that she didn't need to tell us what happened with her mother. From this day forward, she would start new, the past in the past and from this day forward with us. During that time, her daddy got sick and passed away. We escorted her to the funeral, and her mother voiced she didn't want her there, but we knew she needed to say goodbye to her dad. We stood with her in her time of grief. She became part of our family. We were with her at the senior basketball ceremonies, helped her get a class ring and a letter jacket. She and my daughter became sisters and graduated together. Two years later, she fell in love and had the most beautiful wedding as we gave her away to a precious young man.

In August 2014, seven months after my husband passed away, I went to both of these two, sweet young adults who had been so much a part of our family and asked if they would like to be a permanent part of the family. I wanted to adopt them. They were both married and in their 20's, but I still felt very strongly about being their legal and permanent parent. Neither had a parent anymore and I know how lost I felt when my husband died. I'm sure they had a similar lost and lonely, detached feeling. They both agreed and were very excited to officially belong to our family. My other three children agreed and we made it a family decision. In October 2014, we three stood in front of a judge holding hands and they became my legal children. I now have five children. My happiness was complete. My family means so much to me!

I think that sense of 'belonging' is so very important. To have a family, sisters, brothers, parents, whether blood related or not, it matters. Things go wrong between families; miscommunications put wedges between friends; jealous feelings surface between siblings; we must look at ourselves and see what really matters. Christ teaches us that relationships must forgive and grow; giving not always receiving; sometimes sacrificing our own wants.

"And when you stand praying, if you hold anything against anyone, forgive them, so that your Father in heaven may forgive you your sins." - Mark 11:25

When a family is united, and love prevails, contentment sets in like a warm, fuzzy feeling of happiness. It doesn't mean that we all have to agree on everything, but always accept and forgive. We are all so different, but in God's eyes, we are all His children and He accepts us just the way we are, who we are. Surely we can be like Him and offer the same to our own family and friends.

"Happy is the man who finds wisdom, and the man who gains understanding" – Proverbs 3:13

Chapter Six

CONTENTMENT

~ A feeling of calm satisfaction~

Having It All

"If they obey and serve him, they will spend the rest of their days in prosperity and their years in contentment."
-Job 36:11

To have everything you will ever need or want. Wouldn't that be wonderful? We all have desires, but most times we just 'make do' and learn to live with what we have. Being content is a blessing. Always striving, wishing, wanting to obtain things or a life that is really unrealistic brings stress and unhappiness. It's always good to strive for better, but if that's the total focus, then life can lose its purpose.

Here are a few things I find being 'content':

- Sitting on the back screened in porch with a cup of hot coffee or tea…listening to the rustle of trees in the breeze is contentment.
- Doing dishes in the kitchen while listening to my sweetheart practice his guitar and sing in the living room is contentment.
- Riding motorcycles down the backroads, with my Bible in the saddle bag, to church Sunday evenings is contentment.
- Sitting and talking with my aging parents is contentment.
- Holding my sleeping grandbaby, snuggled in my arms is contentment.
- Driving with the windows down with my arm out and singing as loud as I can with my favorite music is contentment.
- Having my children with me, being involved in their lives and just sharing our thoughts and views brings me contentment.

- Reflecting on happy memories, knowing that this life can bring joy is contentment.
- Going to sleep at night, smiling that all is well and that I did my best for the day is contentment.

Finding contentment in living life; that's the key to it all. Having peace in your soul right now, this moment, is contentment. Accepting life as it is in this season, now. Not later in the future after things are better or going to be different, but NOW. No regrets, no wishing or thinking 'could've, should've or would've. Things in the past are the past and can't be changed. Only our future days can reflect on what we do today. Today we accept and smile with the knowledge that happiness comes with being content.

"I rejoice greatly in the Lord that at last you have renewed your concern for me. Indeed, you have been concerned, but you had no opportunity to show it. I am not saying this because I am in need, for I have learned to be content whatever the circumstances. I know what It Is to be in need, and I know what it is to have plenty. I have

learned the secret of being content in any and every situation, whether well fed or hungry, whether living in plenty or in want. I can do everything through him who gives me strength." - Philippians 4:10-13

Chapter Seven

LOVE

~ Feel tender affection for somebody~

The Big Event

"If I speak in the tongues of men or of angels, but do not have ***love****, I am only a resounding gong or a clanging cymbal. If I have the gift of prophecy and can fathom all mysteries and all knowledge, and if I have a faith that can move mountains, but do not have* ***love****, I am nothing. If I give all I possess to the poor and give over my body to hardship that I may boast, but do not have* ***love****, I gain nothing. Love is patient, love is kind. It does not envy, it does not boast, it is not proud. It does not dishonor others, it is not self-seeking, it is not easily angered, it keeps no record of wrongs. Love does not delight in evil but rejoices with the truth. It always protects, always trusts, always hopes, always perseveres. Love never fails. But where there are prophecies, they will cease; where there are tongues, they will be stilled; where there is knowledge, it will pass away. For we know in part and we prophesy in part, but when completeness comes, what is in part disappears. When I was a child, I talked like a child, I thought like a child, I reasoned like a child. When I became a man, I put the ways of childhood behind me. For now we see only a reflection as in a mirror; then we shall see face to face.*

Now I know in part; then I shall know fully, even as I am fully known. And now these three remain: faith, hope and love. But the greatest of these is love."
- 1 Corinthians 13

My son and his girlfriend went to the Gulf Coast of Texas and he proposed at sunset, on the beach. She is such a lovely girl with a spunky personality, perfect for him and greatly approved by this mom. His dad and I went with him to the mall and helped him shop for 'the ring.' Looking back, it was such a privilege to be able to do that with him.

Shortly after the engagement, his dad passed away from cancer. He would not have the privilege to be part of our son's wedding. It broke my son's heart. His dad passed in January and the wedding was to be in October the same year.

As wedding preparations were getting on their way, I kept busy with the planning and excitement of it all. It was to be held at my home! I was going to do my best to make it the biggest event to remember! Since it was scheduled for October, fall colors would accent cream. My list grew: pumpkins (white and orange), corn stalks, fall colored leaves and arrangements and then the menu! Oh, the menu! Bourbon ham, baked mac and cheese, cheesecake and apple spice wedding cake. I made arrangements for a 'wedding tent' to be delivered and set up behind our house. My son dug a fire pit and put bricks that matched the house around it just outside the tent area. We went through the process of selecting tables, chairs, dance floor, lighting…. So much fun and excitement was in the air!

As the Big Day came closer, I realized that involving my 'new friend' was causing some strife between me and my kids. I had met this wonderful man a couple of months earlier and we were enjoying our new found companionship. We shared so much in common (including widowhood) and he was such a strong 'leader' type of personality that I enjoyed him helping with planning the event. He helped build an archway with my son out of tree limbs and wire for the ceremony. He also helped mow and prepare the yard for guests to park. I was having a hard time relating to my kid's attitude and concerns. He was a new friend that had an interest in my happiness. I believe my son was very grateful that he had so much help. My sister and brother-in-law flew in from Seattle and were also a big help.

The wedding tent needed lighting, so we bought several reels of white lights and borrowed some tall ladders so the guys could string them up and across the huge tent. It was so nice seeing everyone pull together to make this event a success! The food was cooking and the decorations and flowers were all prepared.

My three daughters had assignments of what to do and what to make. My other son from Texas arrived and his suit was brushed down and hanging in the sewing room where he and my son were going to be dressing. The bride and her sister and the bridesmaids were going to use the master bedroom.

The evening before, I discovered that my son didn't have a tie to go with his best man suit, so I brought out my husband's entire collection of ties. I still had most of his clothes hanging in the closet. He, my other son, a nephew, son-in-law and my friend all went through the ties looking for the best color to match the theme. We found several, so

I encouraged my friend to wear a nice tie with fall colors and leaves on it also. He was a little nervous about being there at my son's wedding, as I was, but he had helped so much. I wanted to share the joyous event with him even though my daughters were not very happy about it. My sons were very gracious to him and thought that he was a good friend for me. I had no idea about the deep feelings his presence had on my girls.

The wedding day arrived! All parties were dressing, food was being plated and flowers set. Last minute details had us all scrambling, but the special music started, and the groom and best man stood in the beautiful archway and waited for his soon to be bride arrive. She walked from the house down a carpeted pathway with pumpkins lining the sides to the archway. The officiator began and the sweet words of promise, love and commitment were made. My heart was so full I could not hold back the tears. The exchange of rings was the most touching part for me. I gave the bride my husband's wedding band to use in the ceremony. She so graciously received it and then to see her place it on my son's ring finger was almost more than I could bear. Somehow, my husband was there, in the midst of the family and friends approving of this unity. It was so touching.

After pronouncing them husband and wife, the reception that followed was filled with music, food and dancing. All the traditional things followed such as cutting the wedding cake, drinking with arms intertwined together, dancing the first dance and speeches. The evening was as perfect as we could have hoped for. Seeing family and friends that I hadn't seen since my husband's funeral was good too. I introduced my friend to them and they thought he was handsome and nice. I was happy to share this special evening with him. One of my cousins told me that she was happy for me in this season of my life. She was happy that I had found a way to move forward from my loss to find peace and joy. Those words touched me. I didn't know if this new relationship would be a permanent one, but knowing that I was where I was supposed to be in my heart with the loss of my husband, with God's help, I was happy.

Sending my son and new daughter-in-law off to their honeymoon was the final event of the day. The reception went into the late hours of the evening and everyone was winding down and our good-byes were lingering. Hugs and tears were shared as they drove down the narrow, dirt road from the house. Whew! We did it! Now for the clean up….

This wedding was so special. My son was the last of my five children to get married. It is the only one that my husband was unable to physically be there for. In many ways it was sad, but it showed me that life continues to evolve when death comes through to disrupt our lives. No matter what we do, life doesn't 'stand still' but continues forward even though our loved one's life ended. Our lives must continue to share special events, babies, love, laughter and building new memories. Grief cannot be allowed to 'stop' our living.

"Let the morning bring me word of your unfailing love, for I have put my trust in you. Show me the way I should go, for to you I entrust my life". -Psalm 143:8

Chapter Eight

UNCONDITIONAL LOVE

~complete or guaranteed, with no conditions, limitations, or provisos attached~

Reconciliations

"All this is from God, who reconciled us to himself through Christ and gave us the ministry of reconciliation"
-2 Corinthians 5:18

"Bless those who persecute you; bless and do not curse."
-Romans 12:14

I was having trouble with my children understanding that my life was continuing and that I was moving forward. The loss of their dad tore my whole being to a point that thinking and doing was a chore. But I shared with them how God touched me in a personal way and blessed me with a peace and a hope to continue life; my life.

They thought it was too soon for me to date or to see anyone. They thought it was shameful that my new friend wore one of their daddy's ties at my son's wedding. I hadn't even given it a second thought. Their grief was not the same as mine. They were not in the same place on their journey of this loss as I was.

It hurt me terribly that they would think what I was doing was wrong. I had just listened to the minister at my son's wedding say "'til death do us part." Is that true? Am I wrong in finding a new friend? I was thinking that with my husband's wedding ring my son now wears, that he will have as many or more years of marriage as his daddy and I shared. We had almost 35 years of marriage. That's a long time to be with someone and share daily lives with. Being alone is not something I was accustomed to. Even though my husband was in the Navy, we still communicated when he was deployed and we knew it was only a temporary separation. Death is permanent. It's a permanent separation from living. It's a harsh reality, but so very true. He wasn't coming back. I had to manage my life and evolve into something different. Death interrupted our lives and my life had taken a different path. I was on a new journey.

I wrote my children a letter:

~From your Mom and the heart of your Dad ~

Mourning is a tough, emotional setback in our lives. Healing from it is harder than anything I have ever experienced in my entire life. It will always be a continued effort because I believe I lost a part of my life and soul that can never be replaced. My relationship with your Dad was different than the relationship you had. Therefore, our grief experience and healing will be different. I don't expect you to understand what it is to lose a husband/companion/lover and best friend. I too can't quite understand what it is like to lose a Dad. All I know is that we can comfort and love each other. There will be hardships through the changes ahead. Our time, money, careers, homes and relationships will continue to evolve and change for the rest of our lives. Having a heart of acceptance of all these things with each other is our only way of surviving and to hold together our blessed family.

All of our children (your Dad's and mine) are grown and have changed their roles as children to adults. You have your own family unit as God has purposely planned. I am so very happy and proud of all the life companions you have chosen to be with. Each has a love for you and a love for family. I am not going to interfere with your family, but still want to be a role as 'Grandma'. That doesn't mean I will always be available when it is convenient, but will do my best to make sure the Grandma role is achieved. I love my grandkids so much that my heart swells with excitement when I see them!

Choices of our time and choices of our priorities will be different for all of us. What I think would be good choices may not be what you may think are good. We are all in a different place in our lives and have to realize that. Choices to spend time with family get togethers/dinners are strictly up to you. Life's circumstances sometimes consume our decision making, but whatever decisions are made, it's a choice and that choice needs to be dealt with and accepted. My choices right now may not be exactly to your liking, but I feel these are the choices I need to do at this time. I don't feel like my choices are harming anyone, only enhancing my life to be a better person. You may not see it that way, but it is so very true. Remember, we are all in a different place in life...

Here is a portion of a comment that I read daily on 'The Widow's Might.' I have found it to be a comfort and helps with the daily strength I pray for every day:

Life is about moving, not knowing. It's about adapting and changing. It's about taking a single moment and making the best of it; right then-no matter what happens next. When it's over, it's over-the moment is gone. No more second chances or wishes or dreams or could have beens, it's gone. So, take the single moments you are given and live them, RIGHT. Sometimes they will be beautiful, sometimes they will be painful but MOST of the time, they will be both; because, pain and passion are kin.

Don't regret something that once made you smile and brought you joy. Everything in life changes you in some way. If you don't accept the changes you don't accept yourself. Accept you, love you, live the best you – you can be today. Be greater, be wiser, be more than you were yesterday-if you avoid the change, you lose the path and the journey matters.

Choosing happiness and living life with joy should be our purpose with each other as a family. Accepting our differences and loving unconditionally is and should always be part of who we are. Our attitude is a ministry in itself that others can see and feel.

Striving to keep our family at peace has always been something that your Dad and I have worked on diligently. It has been tough at times, but love always prevails. Keep loving and sharing your lives with each other with peace.

I grew up with your Dad. He was my life partner. My plans were broken to grow old with him. I have felt empty and lost. My new friend will never ever replace that relationship. But, he does make me laugh and understands the loss of a life companion. We have cried together, laughed together and just simply sat in silence together knowing it's a 'hard day'. I don't ask you to accept him as anything else except a friend that deserves acknowledgement and respect. He and his family have experienced the same type of loss. Compassion can be a strong healing message.

I will always be your Mom, and your Dad will forever be your Dad. That will never change.

I love you with all my heart and soul. You are a part of who I am and always will be.

~Hugs to you all~

Mom

I love my children so very much and hoped the changes in my life, and theirs weren't meant to be harmful or for spite. But another event in the next months to follow broke my heart. Miscommunication between families can be very hurtful and painful.

Christmas that followed the big wedding was somewhat edgy, but we celebrated at my home that I had decided I needed to sell. It would be the last Christmas together there. We had lived in this home my husband and I built for about 10 years. It was our dream house after traveling the world over with his Navy career. The mortgage payment was more than what I could afford on my paycheck. His Navy retirement for being the surviving spouse was cut by almost half which we didn't know would happen. Then there were utilities and upkeep of a 2400 sq ft home on six acres. I simply could not afford to live in this house. It was becoming more of a burden than my dream home. My children did not want me to sell, but none of them were in a position to purchase it. I HAD to sell.

Maintenance on the house was done to prepare for showing. My new friend was very good at helping out with the list of odd jobs that needed done. During this time, I had my life long friend living with me since my husband's death. I helped her look for a new place with suggestions within her budget. She wasn't happy that I was selling. It seemed that everyone was either unhappy or upset with me all the time. No matter what I said or did, it was always the wrong thing to them. My family was being pulled apart by what they thought I should do and what I knew I had to do.

I can't count the number of nights I cried myself to sleep. My support system from my children was crumbling. I didn't understand how they thought I couldn't move forward with my life. How I was so desperately trying to keep the peace over the grief of my husband's death.
The event was New Year's Eve. My new friend and I had been invited to my brother's house for a full evening of games and food with some of their friends. It sounded like something we should do so we accepted the invitation.

That evening, some of my kids came over and were planning to spend the night and the next day. I told them I had already made plans, but they were welcome to come to the party too. They were not happy about that.

Plans for the next day were already in the works too. My new friend is a Senior Pro Bowler and had a New Year's Day tournament that we planned to attend. I was upset with my kids and my life long friend when they told me I should stay and spend the day with them since this would be the last New Year's Day we would all have in the house. I didn't want to. Things had changed and traditions were not the same. My husband was not going to be there to cook the pot of black eyed peas and cornbread. He wasn't going to be there to watch all the football games and Rose Bowl Parade on the television. Things were different.

I didn't want to be at the house on New Year's Day. I needed to be away, change the tradition to cope with the absence of my husband. Maybe I should have stayed, but it wasn't what was in my heart. I had met someone that treated me with kindness and made me laugh. I needed that. I didn't want to dwell on death and the loss we had endured already for a year. I needed and was ready to move forward. My children were not. Our journey was not the same.

The next day, New Year's Day, I was at the bowling alley, meeting new friends and being in the excitement of the tournament, when I received a text message from my son-in-law. It was a terrible message describing me and my new friend as being shameful and not doing what is expected. It was as if all my kids had come together to send this message out to me. It crushed me like I felt when I lost my husband. The pain of losing my kids took me physically to the floor. I truly had a breakdown out on the front entry to the bowling alley. It was freezing cold with snow on the ground. I simply walked up and down the parking lot crying and practically being in a stupor type of mindset. I could not believe what was happening.

I called my youngest daughter and tried to understand what was going on with them. She tried to explain to me they thought I should be home and it was just too soon for me to be out like this. They needed me to be with them. I was so torn about what I needed to do. I just sat outside in the cold and cried.

I felt that I couldn't go home right away after that. I stayed at my new friend's house for a couple of days. When I did come home, it was after work on a Saturday afternoon and my life long friend had moved out. I had no idea she was planning on this. I went into her empty bedroom and slumped down on the floor and cried. I was so alone. Where had all the love and support from everyone gone? What happened to the unconditional family love? Why did everyone hate me? What did I do wrong? I felt totally alone.

On the first anniversary of my husband's death, I was preparing for installation of new carpet in my house. I had scheduled it that way to keep myself busy. I was cleaning out the pantry, finding old medicine bottles from my husband's illness that had lingered on the back shelf. I sent out some messages to my kids earlier telling them I loved them and was thinking of them on this day. I heard from a couple of them, but what hurt most was that I never heard a comforting message or received a call from my life long friend. She was there with me when my husband passed away, but now it seemed that she had turned away to never be a part of my life again. It was a very difficult day even though I was busy with my house repairs. I found myself out on the front porch, sitting and just crying, alone again. My new friend did come and give me a hug, knowing what day it was and wondering how I was holding up. He had been through it himself just 2 months prior. We both knew how grief would come and visit and stir our hearts. He was a great comfort.

February came and the relationship with my children had not improved. For my birthday, my new friend and I went to Austin, Texas to see my son and his wife. We had a wonderful time seeing the city and sites. It was a short three day weekend, but so worth the effort of the long drive. I had a talk with him about what was going on with the other kids. He told me he supported me and was proud that I could move forward with my life. He didn't understand why some of kids were so adamantly against me making changes. He also 'approved' of my new friend. I felt so relieved when I left knowing that our relationship was stronger and that he knew I was doing the right things for my life.

I had decided to rent a cabin on one of Oklahoma's beautiful lakes for a weekend for me and my children and their families. I made arrangements and called my children that live locally and also my life long friend. I gave them three weeks to arrange their schedules so they could come. I wanted to have a time of healing without the interruptions and knew that getting away from our normal routines would be key.

The weekend came, and only three of my five kids came. My son in Austin Texas wasn't expected to come since I had just been down to see him. I enjoyed the walks through the woods with the grandkids and having a sit down dinner with them all in the evenings. We sat around the big campfire and enjoyed each other's presence. Time had come to talk about the 'elephant' in the center of the room. We discussed the 'whys' of the words and actions that had been on New Year's Day. Trying to understand each other's emotions and working through the real reasons of why they happened. We all learned that sometimes even though we may not agree or understand things, we must always accept things with love and move forward. Forgiveness is a tough thing to accept and give. We achieved reconciliation with one another that day. Unfortunately my life long friend and my other daughter were not there to be a part of the forgiving and healing. It took more time with them on an individual basis and the relationship suffered to the point that recovery has been difficult.

Sometimes the harm that comes through miscommunication and not understanding the situation fully lingers on the heart to the point where forgiveness is difficult. But with God's Grace, it can be done. He forgave those that didn't understand His purpose and hung Him on the cross to die. Surely we should look to Him to help us do the same?

"Then Jesus said, "Father, forgive them, for they do not know what they do." –Luke 23:34

Life demands changes, and how change is dealt with matters. I could have handled things differently, but the decisions I made were based on the future success of moving forward with my life. My family could have done things differently also, but I know change is difficult for everyone. Things won't ever be the same as they were before my husband's death. My family and I can only hold the memories of the past, and not let the past be what motivates our future.

"Carry each other's burdens, and in this way you will fulfill the law of Christ" –Galatians 6:2

What is the Law of Christ?

"A new command I give you: Love one another. As I have loved you, so you must love one another. By this everyone

will know that you are my disciples, if you love one another." –John 13:34-35

Forgiveness; a tough choice to make. It takes positive action and commitment to follow through with change. A change of attitude; change of emotions; change of the heart.

"For if you forgive other people when they sin against you, your heavenly Father will also forgive you."- Matthew 6:4

EPILOGUE

Second Chances

How often do we get a second chance at life? Tragedy strikes and our life feels like it will fall apart and maybe living just seems like it's not even worth it. It takes a lot of courage, strength and determination to move past it. It's a CHOICE to move; step forward; embrace the change. Decisions are extremely hard to make during this time, but making NO decisions is even more harmful.

Relationships change and evolve. How we handle the change determines if the relationship will grow or fail. It takes effort and lots of perseverance. I've learned that relationships are built only if the other party wants to work. Sometimes you can do everything to build the relationship, but it never grows or evolves because the other person just doesn't want to do the work. That's when you love the person, but have to let the relationship rest knowing it won't grow into what you desire. People come into your life for a season. Sometimes the season is short, sometimes it's a lifetime. It can be friends or family.

“Greater love has no one than this, than to lay down one’s life for his friends.” -John 15:13

“And the second, like it, is this: ‘You shall love your neighbor as yourself.’ There is no other commandment greater than these.”-Mark 12:31

We can’t live on the ‘what ifs, should’ve, would’ve’ and look at the past with regrets. We only can live with what today gives us and the decisions of what to do with it. With God’s grace and hope, we can live a bountiful life of love, happiness and joy. Hand in hand with our Heavenly Father is what it takes. Healing is a choice; living with joy is a choice. God gives us second chances to change and move forward. What will you do?

*If it is possible, as much as depends on you, **live** peaceably with all men.” –Romans 12:18*

“And we know that all things work together for good to those who love God, to those who are the called according to His purpose.” –Romans 8:28

-End-

www.ingramcontent.com/pod-product-compliance
Ingram Content Group UK Ltd.
Pitfield, Milton Keynes, MK11 3LW, UK
UKHW040558210726
13854UKWH00008B/1411

9 781387 557653